Foods of
Scandinavia

Barbara Sheen

KIDHAVEN PRESS
A part of Gale, Cengage Learning

Detroit • New York • San Francisco • New Haven, Conn • Waterville, Maine • London

LIBRARY OF CONGRESS CATALOGING-IN-PUBLICATION DATA

Sheen, Barbara.
  Foods of Scandinavia / by Barbara Sheen.
    p. cm. -- (A taste of culture)
  Includes bibliographical references and index.
  ISBN 978-0-7377-4814-7 (hardcover)
  1. Cookery, Scandinavian--Juvenile literature. I. Title.
  TX722.A1S534 2010
  641.5948--dc22

                                                              2009036549

Kidhaven Press
27500 Drake Rd.
Farmington Hills MI 48331

ISBN-13: 978-0-7377-4814-7
ISBN-10: 0-7377-4814-1

Printed in the United States of America
1 2 3 4 5 6 7 14 13 12 11 10

Printed by Bang Printing, Brainerd, MN, 1st Ptg., 02/2010

contents

Days of Darkness, Days of Light

The region of the world known as Scandinavia consists of five nations: Denmark, Finland, Iceland, Norway, and Sweden. These nations are located in the northern part of the Northern Hemisphere, which makes winters here long, cold, and dark. Scandinavia gets from zero to six hours of daylight each day in the winter, with the northern-most locations getting the least light. The cold weather and lack of light makes fishing, farming, and hunting difficult.

Summer, on the other hand, is marked by long hours of daylight and mild weather. In the past, Scandinavians spent most of the summer gathering, preserving, and storing fish, berries, mushrooms, and grains in

FOOD REGIONS OF SCANDINAVIA

BARENTS SEA

ICELAND

Reykjavik

NORWEGIAN SEA

FINLAND

| Fish |
| Crayfish |
| Vegetables |
| Oysters |
| Lobster |
| Pork |
| Prawns |
| Cheese |
| Berries |
| Lamb |
| Cattle |
| Grains |

GULF OF BOTHNIA

RUSSIA

SWEDEN

NORWAY

Oslo

Stockholm

Helsinki

ESTONIA

NORTH SEA

DENMARK

Copenhagen

BALTIC SEA

GERMANY

POLAND

preparation for the winter. Modern Scandinavians no longer have to do this. They can purchase fresh food in supermarkets year-round. But, just like their ancestors, modern Scandinavians still enjoy these tasty staples.

Fish and Seafood

Scandinavia is blessed with long coastlines and thousands of inland waterways. Salmon, herring, eels, oysters, mussels, shrimp, and cod are just a few of the many creatures that make their home in these waters. For many years, fish and seafood were the Scandina-

The Vikings

The Vikings, or Norsemen, lived in Denmark, Sweden, and Norway from the 8th to the 11th century. This time period is known as the age of the Vikings in European history.

The Vikings were expert sailors, warriors, and explorers. They traveled throughout the Atlantic Ocean in longships that were equipped with oars and sails. They traveled as far east as Constantinople (now Istanbul), Turkey, and as far west as Newfoundland, Canada. They raided many towns throughout Europe and established settlements in the British Isles and Europe. They colonized Iceland, Greenland, and Newfoundland. Only the Icelandic colony succeeded. They left writing in the form of runes (poems) in their settlements, describing their lives. They also developed myths and sagas, which are heroic tales about their adventures. These have been passed down for generations.

vian people's main source of protein. In fact, archaeologists believe that the **Vikings** ate fish at every meal.

Today the fishing industry is an important part of every Scandinavian nation's economy. And seafood of all kinds remains a vital part of the Scandinavian people's diet. Scandinavians bake, boil, poach, grill, fry, steam, **cure**, and pickle fish and seafood. They turn it into soft buttery fish balls, crispy croquettes, bubbling casseroles, cold salads, hearty sandwiches, thick milky chowders, hearty stews, creamy spreads, and savory puddings.

Deliciously Preserved

One of Scandinavia's most popular and famous fish dishes is **gravlax** (grav-lax), or cured salmon. In the past Scandinavians preserved salmon for the winter by curing it.

To do this, cooks rub the fish with salt, sugar, and dill. Then they put a weight on the fish and store it in a cool place for at least two days. Before refrigerators were invented, the fish was buried in the cold ground. This process removes all the moisture from the fish and kills any bacteria in it. It also allows the sugar, salt, and dill to blend with the salmon's natural flavor. This makes the salmon taste salty, sweet, and savory all at the same time.

Scandinavians eat gravlax with boiled potatoes and sweet mustard, or on a piece of dense dark bread topped with a slice of green onion. "Gravlax, salmon cured to a velvety silky-smooth texture in a sugar-salt-dill mixture,

Seafood is a staple in the Scandinavian diet. Pictured here is sillsallad, the main ingredient of which is pickled herring.

is one of the great traditional Scandinavian dinners,"[1] explains Swedish chef Marcus Samuelsson.

Herring, another Scandinavian favorite, is salted in much the same way. Then it is marinated or pickled in a solution made of sugar, salt, and vinegar to which ingredients like cloves, carrots, and onions, are added. Scandinavians like combining pickled herring with boiled potatoes, beets, green onions, and hard-boiled eggs to make **sillsallad** (sill-sal-lad). What makes this dish special is that all the ingredients are colored red by the beets.

Gravlax

Gravlax is not difficult to make. It is important to weigh down the salmon to help get the moisture out and to refrigerate it for 48 hours before eating it.

Ingredients
2 salmon fillets, about 8 ounces each
2 tablespoons salt
2 tablespoons sugar
1 tablespoon black pepper, freshly ground
2 tablespoons dill, chopped fresh or dried

Directions
1. Combine the salt, sugar, and pepper in a small bowl, mix.
2. Put one salmon fillet skin side down in a shallow pan or plate. Sprinkle most, but not all, of the dill evenly on the salmon. Then sprinkle on all of the salt, sugar, and pepper mixture.
3. Place the second salmon fillet skin side up on top of the first fillet, so that the seasoning is sandwiched between the fillets. Sprinkle the remaining dill on top.
4. Wrap the salmon in foil. Refrigerate it for 48 hours with a weight, such as a heavy plate or a heavy cutting board, on top of it.
5. Scrape the seasoning off the fillets and cut them into thin slices.
6. Serve with dark bread or rye crisp crackers and sweet mustard.

Serves 4 as an entrée, 8 as an appetizer.

Gravlax, or cured salmon, is one of Scandinavia's most popular fish dishes.

Scandinavians use herring in hundreds of other ways. They pride themselves on their fish dishes. In fact, there are probably as many fish and seafood recipes in Scandinavia as there are cooks. According to writer Kari Diehl, Scandinavians have "turned the preparation of fish and seafood dishes into an art, creating unique recipes that . . . preserve the rich flavors and textures of fish."[2]

Gathering Seasonal Treasures

Cooking with berries and mushrooms is another Scandinavian specialty. Scandinavia has many old forests where a wide variety of berries and mushrooms grow.

Favorite Spices

Scandinavian cooking is not spicy, but it is flavorful. Dill, an herb that grows well in Scandinavia, could be called Scandinavia's national spice. It is grown in almost every Scandinavian garden, sold fresh in Scandinavian shops, and used in a myriad of ways. Dill flavors salted and pickled dishes. Trout, salmon, and herring are rarely cooked without it. Dill is also used in sauces and gravies. It is sprinkled on potatoes and sandwiches. Dill seeds are used in bread and pastries.

Other popular spices are not native to Scandinavia. The Vikings brought spices, like cardamom, ginger, allspice, and cinnamon, to Scandinavia from Constantinople (now Istanbul). These spices are used to flavor cookies, puddings, and meatballs.

Gathering these seasonal treasures is a time-honored tradition. During early fall, people of all ages flock to the countryside to pick berries and mushrooms. The adults teach the children how to distinguish between poisonous and edible mushrooms and berries, and

The tradition of gathering wild mushrooms is as popular in Scandinavia as is apple-picking in the fall in the United States.

everyone has fun spending time together. "Some of my happiest childhood memories recalls days spent walking through fields and forests with my father and grandmother to forage for wild mushrooms,"[3] says Samuelsson.

Wild Mushrooms and Juicy Berries

Scandinavians use mushrooms in many ways. They lightly fry them in butter. They turn them into rich creamy soups, and they chop them and stuff them inside tomatoes or savory tarts. They pickle them, can them, and dry them.

To dry mushrooms, cooks gather about two dozen mushrooms and tie one to another with cord, forming a long strand. Then they put the strands in a warm oven to dry. Scandinavians hang the strands in their kitchens, plucking off a mushroom whenever they need one.

Berries also appear in many Scandinavian dishes. Some berries, like blueberries, strawberries, cranberries, and raspberries, are

Berries of all kinds acccompany many Scandinavian dishes. A popular type is the lingonberry, pictured here.

familiar to Americans, while others like tart red **lingonberries** and tangy golden **cloudberries** are less familiar.

In the past, berries were the Scandinavian people's main source of vitamins A, B, and C. Today Scandinavians can buy fresh fruit imported from other countries in modern supermarkets. Scandinavians eat fresh berries topped with whipped cream and sugar. They make cold and hot fruit soups, nourishing juices, and incredibly rich and thick puddings with them. They add them to omelets and sprinkle them on pancakes and waffles. And they preserve them for winter in sweet and tangy jams, relishes, syrups, and sauces that they eat with meatballs, game meat, chicken, and fried fish. "When fresh produce . . . are in season, they are prized and served in abundance," explains Finnish cook and author Taimi Previdi. "Almost every household does some preserving for winter."[4]

Hearty Grains

Scandinavians also add berries to pies, cakes, breads, muffins, and **porridges**, foods made with the many grains Scandinavians have always enjoyed. Rye and oats are especially popular. These sturdy grains have a short growing season and thrive in cool climates. In fact, rye first appeared as a weed in Scandinavia. When farmers saw how it survived when wheat failed, they began cultivating it. By the Middle Ages, rye bread had become a staple on Scandinavian tables. It is served for breakfast, lunch, and dinner. According to *The Best*

Scandinavian rye bread is very hearty and is typically served with all meals.

of Scan Fest, a book of recipes contributed by many Scandinavian cooks, "no meal is complete without rye bread."[5]

Scandinavian rye bread is dark, dense, and slightly sour. It has a hearty flavor and is loaded with protein and fiber. It resists spoiling and can be stored for months. Since breadmaking is time consuming and the bread did not spoil easily, in the past, Scandinavian housewives would bake dozens of loaves at a time. That way they did not have to bake bread often. They

Oat Porridge with Strawberry Preserves

Oat porridge is easy to make. For a more authentic taste, use old-fashioned oats rather than instant oatmeal.

Ingredients

1 cup milk
1 cup water
1 cup oats
2 pats butter
2 teaspoons strawberry preserves

Directions

1. Put the milk and water in a pot and bring it to a boil.
2. Stir in the oats. Lower the heat to medium and cook for 5 minutes, stirring frequently.
3. Divide the oats into two bowls. Top each with a pat of butter, a teaspoon of preserves, and a splash of milk.

Serves 2.

A hot bowl of porridge, also known as oatmeal, is a common breakfast food in Scandinavia.

hung the loaves, which were round with a large whole in the middle, from poles suspended from the ceiling of their kitchen. Today most Scandinavians buy rye bread at bakeries and supermarkets.

Flatbreads and **rusks** are other tasty Scandinavian favorites that are made with rye flour. Both can be stored indefinitely without spoiling. Flatbreads are breads that have been left to dry out. They have a pebbly texture and are like crackers. Rusks are hard, twice-baked breads and buns. "Rusks are made by splitting soft . . . buns into two parts, then baking them again until they are crisp. They are delicious spread with butter and honey. . . . Finns and Swedes fill big jars with rusks,"[6] explains author Beatrice Ojakangas.

Rye and oats are also used to make porridges. Porridges are served for breakfast and for dinner. Oatmeal, in particular, is very popular. It provides warmth and energy, making it a perfect way to start a cold Scandinavian day. In addition to cooking it on the stovetop, Scandinavians like to bake oatmeal overnight at a low temperature then serve it steaming hot in the morning. They top it with milk, lingonberry or strawberry preserves, and a pat of butter. The result is hot, sweet, creamy, and simply delicious.

It is no wonder Scandinavians like oats. In the past, they depended on oats, rye, fish, seafood, berries, and mushrooms to survive their harsh winters. Today they turn to these foods, not out of necessity, but because they are delicious.

Favorite Foods

Scandinavian cooks do not like to waste food. In the past, they faced food shortages during especially harsh winters and times of war. Out of necessity, Scandinavian cooks developed creative and delicious recipes that utilized leftovers and fillers. The dishes they created were practical, thrifty, and hearty. Among their favorites are sandwiches, pea soup, pancakes, and meatballs.

Thrifty Delicacies

Scandinavians love **smorrebrods** (smor-re-broths), thick open-faced sandwiches, piled so high with toppings that they have to be eaten with a knife and fork. "Smorrebrods are not dainty," explains food writer Re-

Progressive Nations

The nations of Scandinavia are Denmark, Finland, Iceland, Norway, and Sweden. These nations are often called the most progressive in the world. They favor laws that improve the quality of life of their citizens. Scandinavians have excellent health care and long life expectancies. All five nations boast strong economies that encourage scientific research and high literacy rates. In fact, Sweden has the highest literacy rate in the world.

The nations of Scandinavia are also quite environmentally conscious. They have instituted many energy-reduction practices and have low greenhouse emissions.

They are also known for their strong support of civil rights. They were among the world's earliest nations to give women the same rights as men. During World War II, the people of Denmark showed great bravery in trying to protect their Jewish population from the Nazis.

Denmark, Finland, Iceland, Norway, and Sweden are also some of the largest providers of financial aid to developing nations.

gina Schrambling. "These are knife-and-fork extravaganzas: the meat flops off the brown bread, the fried plaice [fish] covers not just the bread but the entire plate."[7]

Scandinavians have been eating the sandwiches since the late 1800s, when a Danish merchant came up with the idea of making and selling the open-faced treats to hungry workers from the back of a wagon. Today the sandwiches are sold everywhere from little cafés to fine restaurants. And they are a popular homemade

Extremely thick sandwiches made up of various fillings are a well known meal in Scandinavia.

meal. Smorrebrods are a traditional Saturday night dinner in much of Scandinavia. They are also popular for appetizers, lunches, and snacks.

A smorrebrod usually starts with a thinly sliced piece of dark bread slathered with butter. In fact, the word *smorrebrod* literally means "buttered bread." Next comes a lettuce leaf. Then the artistry begins. What follows is only limited by the cook's imagination. Almost any foods make delicious toppings. In fact, one Copenhagen, Denmark, restaurant offers 300 different types of smorrebrods. The sandwiches can be simple or elaborate. There are no rules or exact measurements,

Roast Beef Smorrebrod

Open-faced roast beef sandwiches are very popular throughout Scandinavia. Ham, turkey, or chicken can be used instead of roast beef and cheese, cucumber, onions, and green pepper slices can also be added.

Ingredients
2 slices dark rye or pumpernickel bread
2 teaspoons soft butter
4 slices roast beef, cut thin but not shaved
6 thin slices tomato
2 hard-boiled eggs, sliced
2 teaspoons fresh dill
2 large lettuce leaves

Directions
1. Butter one side of each slice of bread.
2. Put a lettuce leaf on each slice of bread.
3. Put 2 slices of roast beef on top of the lettuce on each slice of bread.
4. Arrange the hard-boiled egg slices on top of the roast beef using one egg per slice of bread.
5. Add 3 tomato slices to each smorrebrod, sprinkle with dill.
Serves 2.

which make smorrebrods a good way to use leftovers. "Like a patchwork quilt, it is frequently made of leftovers. Sliced cooked meats, such as roast chicken, beef, or pork roast or chops, sautéed apples and onions, smoked salmon, boiled shrimp, cucumber salad . . . the list goes on and on,"[8] says author Beatrice Ojakangas.

Ham, scrambled eggs, and onions make a smorrebrod. So does gravlax, cream cheese, and cucumber, or herring, potatoes, and chives. The possibilities are endless. Once the toppings have been selected, the sandwich is crowned with a sprig of dill or parsley so that the smorrebrod looks as tempting as it tastes, which is why *The Best of Scan Fest* describes smorrebrods as "artistic and edible works of art."[9]

A Weekly Treat

Pea soup is another Scandinavian favorite. It may not be as pretty to look at as a smorrebrod, but it tastes just as delicious. The hearty soup has been a mainstay of Scandinavian cooking as far back as the Middle Ages, when dried peas were a staple cold-weather food for much of northern Europe. During World War II, when food was scarce, the Finnish army was fed mainly on pea soup. "It has been said that the Finnish army ran on pea soup, and it may be true,"[10] says Finnish cook and author Taimi Previdi. Farmworkers, too, depended on it in times of scarcities.

Modern Scandinavians no longer eat pea soup out of necessity. They eat it because they love it. It is usually served as the main course for lunch or dinner every Thursday throughout the winter. This custom began in the 1400s when many religious Scandinavians fasted on Friday. To prepare for the fast, they ate a hearty meal of pea soup because it stuck with them. Swedish chef Marcus Samuelsson recalls, "The soup appeared

Pea Soup

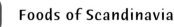

Pea soup is not difficult to make, but it does take time. Green or yellow split peas can be used. The soup can also be made without ham and with salt to taste. In this recipe the potato is cleaned but not peeled. The potato can be peeled if preferred.

Ingredients
1 pound dried split peas
2 quarts water
1 pound ham hock or shoulder
1 onion, peeled and chopped
1 large carrot, peeled and chopped
1 celery stalk, chopped
1 small potato, cleaned and diced
1/2 teaspoon pepper
1/2 teaspoon marjoram
1/2 teaspoon thyme
1/2 teaspoon ginger

Directions
1. Put the peas and water in a pot. Soak the peas overnight.
2. Add all the other ingredients to the pot. Bring it to a boil. Reduce the heat to low, cover the pot, and cook about 1.5 to 2 hours, stirring occasionally. It is done when the peas and meat are tender.
3. Remove the meat from the pot. Remove the bone from the meat. Cut the meat into bite-size pieces and put them in the soup.
4. Serve with bread and butter.
Serves 4 to 8.

on our table every Thursday night throughout the long winter, which lasted from mid September to March . . . .

Every Wednesday night, my grandma would begin her preparations for the next night's dinner by soaking the peas."[11]

The soup is often called both Sweden's and Finland's national dish. People of all walks of life enjoy it. In fact, it was said to be the favorite dish of Sweden's King Gustav V.

Besides tasting wonderful, the soup is hearty, economical, and nutritious. It is made with dried yellow or green peas. The peas are slowly cooked in water along with salted ham or a ham bone and vegetables like onions and carrots. Other leftover vegetables are tossed

Thick and delicious pea soup is most welcome on a cold winter's night, but Scandinavians enjoy it all year 'round.

in, too. Spices, such as ginger, thyme, and black pepper, may be added for extra flavor. Slow cooking gives the different flavors a chance to intermingle.

The soup is ready when it is almost as thick as pudding. It is served steamy hot with a spoonful of grainy mustard on top and flatbread on the side. The meat and vegetables may be served in the soup or removed from the soup and served on the side. Either way, Scandinavian pea soup is rich and creamy with a comforting taste that is hearty and filling. It is the perfect way to warm a body on a cold, dark, winter day.

And Pancakes, Too

Traditionally a dessert of pancakes follows Thursday's pea soup. Pancakes are also served as a side dish or a light dinner on other days of the week.

Scandinavians love pancakes, and they take them quite seriously. Not just any pancakes will do. Scandinavians insist that their pancakes be paper-thin and incredibly light. According to Ojakangas, they must be "so light that Swedes say they should fly off the griddle."[12]

More like delicate French crepes than thick, fluffy American pancakes, Scandinavian pancakes may be as large as a dinner plate, or as small as a silver dollar. To make the smaller-size cakes, cooks use a special cast-iron pan known as a **plattar pan** (plat-tar pan). It has seven circular depressions that are about 3 inches (7.6cm) in diameter each. Cooks pour the batter into the depressions, which allows them to make seven perfectly shaped pancakes all at the same time. Previdi

Large, thin pancakes fried in cast iron skillets are a popular dish in Scandinavia.

says, "Almost every household in Finland has one of these cast iron skillets for making pancakes."[13]

The batter is typically made with flour, eggs, and milk. But it may also be made with leftover porridge or rice pudding. Once the pancakes are hot and golden, smaller pancakes are stacked. Larger ones are folded in quarters and wrapped around whipped cream and lingonberry preserves and topped with powdered sugar. Or, if the pancakes are being eaten as a light meal or a side dish, they may be rolled around ham and cheese or leftover fish.

Meatballs

Meatballs are another economical Scandinavian favorite. Swedish meatballs are famous around the world. But meatballs are not just a Swedish specialty. Cooks

Reindeer Meat

Wild herds of reindeer live in Norway. These animals have been hunted here since the Ice Age.

The Sami, a Scandinavian ethnic group that lives in far northern Sweden, Finland, Norway, and Russia, also raise reindeer for meat.

The meat is low in fat and high in protein. It is tender and tastes similar to venison (deer meat). Reindeer meatballs are popular in Scandinavia. They are sold ready-made in cans. Reindeer sausage is popular in Finland. Smoked reindeer and reindeer steaks are also available throughout Scandinavia.

Perhaps the best known dish to come from Scandinavia is meatballs. They are a favorite across Scandinavia and are served in many varieties.

throughout Scandinavia make them. It is a good way to use leftovers. As a result, there are countless ways to make meatballs.

Scandinavian meatballs are made with beef, pork, or veal in combination or alone. The meat is mixed with breadcrumbs, mashed potatoes, flour, butter, eggs, milk, and cream or beef broth, and flavored with dried mustard, dried nutmeg, dried onions, and allspice, or with just a pinch of white pepper. The meatballs may be as big as a golf ball or as small as a coin.

What they are served with also varies. They may be

topped with brown gravy, cream sauce, or pan drippings, and accompanied by lingonberry preserves, pickled cucumbers, wide noodles, rice, or mashed potatoes. They may be served hot or cold.

No matter the recipe or the accompaniments, one thing is the same throughout Scandinavia: Almost everyone likes meatballs. Danish American cook Janis Andersen explains, "It is a national dish in Denmark . . . in fact, one might have reason to say frikadeller [Danish for meatballs] is the Danes favorite dish of all."[14]

Like great artists, Scandinavian cooks have a knack for transforming leftovers into unique and delicious dishes like meatballs. Meatballs, pancakes, smorrebrods, and pea soup are Scandinavian masterpieces. It is no wonder they are among the Scandinavian people's favorite foods.

Chapter 3

Going Out for Coffee

Scandinavians love to snack. **Fika** (fee-kah), which means "going out for coffee" is an essential part of Scandinavian life. Charming cafés that serve strong coffee in dainty little cups accompanied by delicious baked goods are everywhere. Taking a break to meet friends at a café gives busy Scandinavians a chance to relax while enjoying a steaming cup of coffee and a buttery pastry. In fact, the people of Finland drink more coffee than any other people in the world. And most businesses in Scandinavia encourage workers to take a midmorning coffee break and an afternoon coffee break. "No one takes their coffee breaks as seriously as Scandinavians," says writer Kari Diehl. "Part of the daily ritual, especially in Sweden, is to fika, go out for

Many Scandinavians find time each day to take a break from work and enjoy coffee and sweets at one of the many sidewalk cafes.

coffee every two hours or so. Friends generally meet at a café where they'll order snacks such as cinnamon rolls, rusks, and sweet yeasted breads."[15]

Coffee Breads

Scandinavians are wonderful bakers. Coffee breads are a regional specialty. Every café serves these semisweet, spicy treats, which as their name implies, are a perfect complement to coffee. Coffee breads are yeast breads laced with dried fruit and flavored with **cardamom**. It is the cardamom that gives the bread its subtly spiced flavor.

Scandinavians have been using cardamom in their

baking since the Vikings brought it to Scandinavia from Turkey more than 1,000 years ago. The spice, which originated in India, has an enticing warm fragrance and a delicate taste similar to ginger. "When I taste cardamom in a bread, cookie or cake, I immediately assume it's a Scandinavian recipe. The smell of cardamom rising from the oven is enough to make me homesick for my mother's or grandmother's cooking! Cardamom gives a unique taste and aroma to Swedish and other Scandinavian baked goods,"[16] explains a writer on the Web site, Scandinavian Cooking.

Coffee breads come in many shapes and sizes. There are large rings, small buns, and long braided loaves. Most contain raisins. Some also contain sweet bits of orange peel. Almonds, apples, and cinnamon, too, find

A Coffee Table

Besides going out for coffee, inviting guests for a late afternoon "coffee table" is a popular way of entertaining in Scandinavia. Coffee is served along with tea and soft drinks. Traditionally seven sweets are laid out on the table with the beverages. Seven is considered a lucky number in Scandinavia.

The sweets are likely to include Danish, coffee bread, almond-flavored rusk, cream cake, appelkaka, cookies, and chocolate balls. Chocolate balls taste similar to fudge. They are made by rolling a mix of oats, sugar, cocoa, butter, and coffee into walnut-size balls, which are decorated with pearl sugar or coconut.

These pastries topped with pearl sugar are an example of the many coffee breads enjoyed by Scandinavians.

their way into coffee bread. And although coffee bread contains sugar, it is not overly sweet.

The crust has a golden sheen that comes from brushing the top of the bread with egg before putting it in the oven. After the bread comes out of the oven, the crust is sprinkled with pearl sugar, a type of coarse sugar about 0.08 inches (0.2cm) in diameter that does not melt on top of the bread, but rather decorates it like salt on a pretzel. The bread itself is soft and fluffy. It tastes wonderful plain or spread with butter or jam.

Buttery Pastry

Sweet, light, buttery pastries are another fika favorite. Known as Danish in most of the world, these pastries are made throughout Scandinavia, but the Danish variety is the most well-known. It takes a lot of skill to make these pastries. The dough, which is spiced with sugar, cardamom, and cinnamon, is rolled out and coated with sweet rich butter. Then it is folded into layers and rolled out again and again. This process is repeated until the dough is incredibly thin and buttery. Austrian bakers, hired to replace striking Danish bakers in the 1840s, brought this method of working with dough to Denmark. The results were creamy, flaky, deliciously crisp, puff pastries that melt in the mouth. When the strike ended, Danish bakers adopted the method of rolling butter between layers of dough. Soon bakeries throughout Scandinavia followed.

Bakeries and cafés entice passersby with Danish, which are shaped into bear claws, fat braids, triangu-

Danish pastry is known worldwide for its light, buttery layers of dough and sweet fillings.

lar turnovers, plump squares, and swirled pinwheels. They are often filled with sweet vanilla-butter cream, berry jam, sweet cheese, or fruit, which oozes out with each bite. A coffee glaze, made with coffee, butter, and powdered sugar, gives the pastries a glistening crown. They may also be topped with chocolate. According to author Beatrice Ojakangas, "window shopping in Denmark can send a pastry addict into euphoria [extreme joy]. Shelves in the windows of every baker's shop are filled with variation upon variation of treats made with sweet, flaky, yeast-risen Danish pastry dough."[17]

Simple Danish Cheese Pastry

Danish pastry is difficult to make from scratch. This recipe uses refrigerated crescent roll dough instead of homemade pastry. Fruit preserves may be substituted for the cheese filling or some preserves may be mixed in with the cheese filling.

Ingredients
2 cans refrigerated crescent roll dough
8 ounces cream cheese, softened
1 egg, separated
1/2 cup + 2 tablespoons sugar
1 teaspoon vanilla
2 teaspoon cinnamon
1 teaspoon water

Directions
1. Preheat the oven to 350°F.
2. Spray a 9 x 13 inch baking pan with nonstick spray. Spread 1 can of crescent roll dough on the bottom of the pan. Pinch the seams together to seal the pastry.
3. Mix together the cream cheese, 1/2 cup of the sugar, 1 teaspoon of the cinnamon, the vanilla, and the egg yolk. Spread the mixture over the pastry.
4. Spread the other can of crescent roll dough on top. Press on the ends and corners to seal.
5. Mix the egg white and water and thinly brush over the dough. Some should be leftover. Mix the rest of the cinnamon and the sugar and sprinkle on top.
6. Bake 20 to 30 minutes until golden.
7. Let the pastry cool. Cut it into squares.
Serves 10 to 12.

Fun Candies

Colorful gummy candies are very popular in Scandinavia. Similar to gumdrops, these sweet and chewy candies come in fun shapes, like elephants, rats, starfish, sea horses, whales, fish, coins, boats, and cars. Swedish gummy fish are the most famous.

Shoppers serve themselves by filling little paper bags with the candies, which are stored in bins in candy shops. They pay for the candy according to weight.

It is common to see people pulling the candies out of the little bags and popping the treats into their mouths on Scandinavian streets. The candies come in a variety of fruit flavors, which match their color. For instance, yellow fish are lemon flavored. The exception is the black fish. They taste salty rather than sweet.

Swedish gummy fish are a fun treat.

Delicious Cakes

Rich cakes crowned with sugar, frosting, or whipped cream are another fika tradition. Apple cakes, spice cakes, cream cakes, and chocolate cakes are just a few of the many delectable offerings.

Appelkaka (ep-pel kah-kah), or apple cake, is a

popular favorite. It is a very simple cake, traditionally made with leftover breadcrumbs. The breadcrumbs, mixed with vanilla and sugar, are lightly toasted and layered between apple sauce or apple slices coated with butter, cinnamon, and sugar. Or the breadcrumbs may be spread on the bottom of a cake pan and topped with a buttery cake batter and crowned with apple slices. Either way, the cake is baked until it is golden. Then it is decorated with sugar sprinkled on the top in a lacy

pattern. To make the pattern, bakers cut folded paper in much the same way young children cut paper to make paper snowflakes. In fact, cutting the paper pattern is often the job of a young family member. The pattern is held above the cooled cake and sugar is sifted through the holes. Thick, rich,

A Swedish cream cake topped with strawberries.

Strawberry Cream Cake

This recipe uses packaged yellow cake mix to make it quick and easy. White or chocolate cake mix may also be used. Use two 8- or 9-inch round pans of equal size and shape. Nonstick pans are especially good, because it is easy to remove the cake from them.

Ingredients
1 box yellow cake mix (18.25 oz.)
2 cups whipped topping or whipped cream
1 teaspoon vanilla extract
2 tablespoons sugar
1 quart strawberries, cleaned and sliced

Directions
1. Prepare the yellow cake mix following the package directions. Spray the pans with nonstick spray. Divide the batter between the two pans. Bake as directed on the package.
2. Cool the cakes.
3. Mix the whipped topping, sugar, and vanilla.
4. When the cakes are cool, remove them from the pans. Put one cake on a plate. Slice the rounded top off, so the top of the cake is flat. Spread half the whipped cream on the flattened top, then put half the strawberries on top of the whipped cream.
5. Put the second cake, flat side down, on top of the strawberries. Spread the rest of the whipped cream and then the strawberries on top of the second cake.

The cake can be served immediately or it can be refrigerated for an hour before serving.

Makes one cake. Serves 12.

vanilla custard sauce, made with whipped cream, eggs, vanilla, and sugar, is often served on the side. "Whether served alone . . . or with vanilla sauce, appelkaka is a treat,"[18] says Diehl.

Cream cakes are another treat. Most of these cakes begin as two layers of marvelously moist, spongy yellow cake. The bottom layer is topped with whipped cream and fresh strawberries, bananas, or other fruit. Then the second layer is added. It is topped with whipped cream, fruit, sugar, and nuts. One Icelandic cook says, "These creations are as beautiful and tempting to behold as they are delicious and fattening!"[19]

Fit for a Princess

Princess cake, a colorful and elaborate three-layer cream cake, is yet another fika temptation. According to a Swedish legend, the cake was named after three Swedish princesses, Margareta, Martha, and Astrid, whose cooking teacher created the cake just for them in the 1920s. Each layer of this fluffy sponge cake is topped with vanilla cream, raspberry jam, and fresh whipped cream. The whipped cream is piled especially high in the middle of the top cake layer, which gives the cake its unique dome shape.

The whole cake is covered with **marzipan**. It is a sweet paste made with ground almonds, sugar, and eggs. It is as soft and pliable as clay, so it can be easily molded into different shapes. For princess cake, it is colored with mint-green food coloring, rolled out like piecrust, and draped over the cake. The marzipan is

Slices of princess cake are as tasty as they are beautiful.

usually decorated with sugar and pink marzipan roses, or actual roses. Author Jerry Anne Di Vecchio calls the cake "a royal treat. . . . The name is fitting; that's precisely how you feel when dessert is served."[20]

Princess cake, cream cakes, appelkaka, Danish, and coffee breads are all fit for a king or a queen. Served with coffee these treats are hard to resist. That is why they are a fika tradition.

Celebrating with Food

Scandinavians love to get together with friends and family and celebrate with special foods throughout the year. Christmas is an especially festive time filled with holiday cookies and special foods. But it does not have to be Christmas for Scandinavians to celebrate. No matter the time of year, huge buffets known as **smorgasbords** (smor-gahs-bords) are served for special occasions.

Christmas Cookies

Christmas in Scandinavia is a joyous time. Many Scandinavians start getting ready for the holiday at least a month in advance. Making cookie dough, which is usually frozen until right before Christmas, is a first step. It

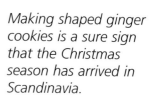

Making shaped ginger cookies is a sure sign that the Christmas season has arrived in Scandinavia.

is not uncommon for Scandinavian bakers to make many different kinds of cookies, which they serve on pretty platters to guests throughout the holiday season. The cookies are also hung as holiday decorations, perfuming Scandinavian homes with their sweet zesty aroma. "For my grandmother . . . preparations for Christmas began in October," Swedish chef Marcus Samuelsson recalls. "She would make batches of dough for ginger cookies and other Christmas cookies and freeze them. By the time she finished, it was already December."[21]

Pepparkakar (pep-pahr-kah-kahr), wonderfully spicy pig-shaped ginger cookies, are among everyone's favorites. It would not be Christmas without them. According to author Beatrice Ojakangas, "these cookies appear in bakeries and food markets all over . . . beginning in Advent [the fourth Sunday before Christmas]. When children see these decorated pig-shaped cookies, they know the Christmas season has arrived."[22]

No one knows for sure why the cookies are shaped like pigs. Years ago most Scandinavian families raised a pig that they slaughtered for Christmas dinner. Although this is no longer a common practice, it may be that the cookie's shape represents these pigs.

Pepparkakar tastes like gingersnaps. To make them shiny, the cookies are usually painted with egg before baking. Once they cool, a child's name or the word

Santa Claus's Headquarters

According to Finnish legend, the original Santa Claus lived in Rovaniemi, Finland, a village in the Arctic Circle. Based on this legend, the Finnish people have constructed a special village and park in Rovaniemi.

The village is like a theme park. Tourists can visit Santa Claus's home and office. They can meet and talk to Santa and Mrs. Claus every day of the year. They can see an exhibit on Christmas traditions throughout the world, as well as a replica of the elves' toy factory.

The park has activities for children and a special area for reindeer. There are lots of restaurants and souvenir shops. There is also a post office where mail addressed to Santa's Headquarters is forwarded. Tourists from all over the world visit the village and park.

nissu (nis-soo), which means "Christmas Pig" in Swedish, is written in icing on the cookies. Faith Adiele, who grew up in Finland, recalls, "My Finnish grandmother and I spent all December at the kitchen table cutting out nissu, little Swedish pigs. . . . Before baking, we painted them with tiny brushes. . . . Sheet after sheet emerged from the oven transformed, the egg paint set into a deep satiny glaze."[23]

Scandinavian bakers make ginger cookies in other shapes, too. Gingerbread people, hearts, and horses are also popular at Christmas. So are **krumkakers** (krum-kah-kers), large, thin, cone-shaped cookies. Bakers make these delicate cookies one at a time in a special iron known as a **krumkaker iron**. It works like a waffle iron.

The iron is made of two cast-iron plates, each measuring about 5 inches (12.7cm) in diameter. They are hinged together and imprinted with a floral pattern. When the baker pours the cookie batter on the bottom plate and shuts the iron, the floral design is imprinted on the cookie. The hot cookie, which is soft and pliable, is rolled into a cone. As it cools, it becomes crisp. Then cooks fill the krumkaker with whipped cream mixed with berry jam. According to *The Best of Scan Fest*, "krumkaker is never missing from a Norwegian Christmas party."[24]

Christmas Dinner

Christmas cookies are served throughout the holiday season, while Christmas dinner is served on Christ-

Lutefisk is one dish certain to be found at Christmas dinner in Scandinavia.

mas Eve. It is a huge feast that goes on for hours. In the past, the food was left out all night to feed the elves and gnomes who Scandinavians believed lived in their gardens and guarded their homes. This may be where the practice of leaving cookies and milk out for Santa Claus originated.

Christmas dinner menus vary depending on local traditions, but certain foods are likely to be found on every Christmas table throughout Scandinavia. These foods have been part of Scandinavian Christmas celebrations for centuries.

Lutefisk (loot-fisk) is one such food. It is dried salted codfish. Before it is served, it is soaked in water for hours. This washes away the salt and makes the fish, which becomes quite hard when it is dried, as soft as butter. Then it is boiled or baked and served with mustard, melted butter, or cream sauce.

Sugar cured ham topped with breadcrumbs and mustard and baked until it is tender is another Christmas favorite. Before it is served, the cook writes "Merry Christmas" across the top in white icing and decorates it with baked apples, orange slices, and cooked prunes.

Traditionally **glogg** (glook) is served with the meal. It is a spiced punch made with wine, sugar, ginger, orange rinds, cinnamon, cardamom, cloves, and aquavit, an alcoholic beverage that is produced in Scandinavia. Nonalcoholic glogg, made with fruit juice and spices, is served to children and adults who do not drink alcoholic beverages. Glogg is poured into mugs containing raisins and almonds and served steaming hot.

Glogg

Here is a recipe for glogg that everyone can enjoy. It is easy to make. Cranberry juice can be substituted for grape juice.

Ingredients

4 cups apple juice or cider
1 cup grape juice
1/2 orange, peeled and chopped
1/8 cup sugar
1 cinnamon stick
1 teaspoon cloves
1/3 cup raisins
1/3 cup almonds, blanched and slivered

Directions

1. Put all the ingredients in a large pot. Bring to a boil.
2. Lower the heat. Cook on low for 30 minutes.
3. Strain the glogg into six cups or mugs. Add a few raisins and almonds to each. Serve hot.

Serves 6.

Glogg is a hot, spiced wine drink traditionally served at Christmas dinner.

An almond is also dropped in the Christmas porridge, a favorite Christmas dessert. Finding the almond is almost as much fun as eating the sweet cereal. Whoever finds it is supposed to have good luck in the coming year. And if a single woman finds it, it is believed she will get married by next Christmas.

Smorgasbord

No matter what else is served, Christmas dinner almost always begins with a smorgasbord. The term *smorgasbord* literally means "bread and butter table." But a smorgasbord consists of more than just bread and butter. It is many hot and cold appetizers, including bread and butter, which are placed on a long table from which guests serve themselves. Although a typical smorgasbord includes more than enough food to constitute a feast, it is served as the prelude to a large sit-down meal. Other special occasions, like New Year's Eve dinner and wedding receptions, almost always start with a smorgasbord.

A smorgasbord is designed to be eaten over several hours. Guests take breaks between courses to visit and sing traditional songs. Typically food at a smorgasbord is eaten in a certain order. First is pickled herring. Other cold fish and meat dishes, like gravlax and roast beef, follow. Cold salads and hard-boiled eggs come next. Then come hot dishes, such as meatballs. Cheese is last. All the food is eaten with, or on, bread and butter. Guests get a fresh plate for each course. They do not overeat, because they want to leave room for the meal

Cucumber Salad

This cold salad, known as *agurkesalat* in Denmark, is often part of a smorgasbord. It is easy to make.

Ingredients
1 large cucumber, peeled
1/2 cup water
1/2 cup white vinegar
1/4 cup sugar
1/4 teaspoon pepper
1/4 teaspoon salt

Directions
1. Combine all the ingredients except the cucumber in a large bowl. Stir well.
2. Cut the cucumber into thin round slices. Add the cucumber to the bowl. Stir.
3. Refrigerate overnight.
4. Drain the liquid and serve.

Serves 6.

Cucumber salad is a light, simple side dish.

that follows. According to Ojakangas, "there is a definite order to feeding oneself at a smorgasbord. Food is never heaped on the plate. The idea is to sample the foods a few at a time, making several trips to the table. This keeps the various flavors separate and distinct."[25]

The number of foods in each category determines the size of the smorgasbord. Home smorgasbords are usually smaller than those in restaurants, which offer mountains of food. For instance, some restaurants offer ten varieties of cheeses and pickled herring, while guests are likely to find two or three varieties of these dishes in home smorgasbords.

The smorgasbord originated in 16th-century Sweden among Swedish royalty, where it was known as a snaps table. But it also has practical roots. Long ago, Scandinavians traveled long distances by horse and

A smorgasbord offers a great many appetizer foods, which are meant for people to snack on over the course of several hours, all leading up to the main sit-down meal.

Special Days

Scandinavians celebrate many special days. Midsummer's Day, which commemorates the longest day of the year, is celebrated throughout Scandinavia. On this day, Scandinavians decorate their houses with wreathes and flowers. They usually eat fish, boiled potatoes, and cream pudding. On Midsummer's Eve, people light bonfires.

On December 13, Scandinavians celebrate Saint Lucia's Day. At this dark time of year, Scandinavians look forward to the coming of spring and the return of the sun. To celebrate, a girl is chosen to portray Saint Lucia. She wears a white gown and a crown made of red berries and lit candles. Other girls carrying lit candles walk behind her. Saint Lucia carries a tray of special buns. They are made with saffron, a yellow spice, which turns the buns yellow, like little suns.

buggy or horse-drawn sleighs to church on Sunday. By the time services ended, everyone was hungry. So each family brought food to share. It was spread out on a long table for everyone to serve themselves just as modern smorgasbords are laid out. And just like today, nobody walked away hungry.

Clearly when Scandinavians celebrate, there is always plenty of food. Holiday cookies, special Christmas dishes, and celebratory smorgasbords not only fill hungry stomachs, but they also make holidays and special occasions more memorable.

Metric Conversions

Mass (weight)

1 ounce (oz.)	= 28.0 grams (g)
8 ounces	= 227.0 grams
1 pound (lb.) or 16 ounces	= 0.45 kilograms (kg)
2.2 pounds	= 1.0 kilogram

Liquid Volume

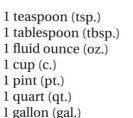

1 teaspoon (tsp.)	= 5.0 milliliters (ml)
1 tablespoon (tbsp.)	= 15.0 milliliters
1 fluid ounce (oz.)	= 30.0 milliliters
1 cup (c.)	= 240 milliliters
1 pint (pt.)	= 480 milliliters
1 quart (qt.)	= 0.96 liters (l)
1 gallon (gal.)	= 3.84 liters

Pan Sizes

8- inch cake pan	= 20 x 4-centimeter cake pan
9-inch cake pan	= 23 x 3.5-centimeter cake pan
11 x 7-inch baking pan	= 28 x 18-centimeter baking pan
13 x 9-inch baking pan	= 32.5 x 23-centimeter baking pan
9 x 5-inch loaf pan	= 23 x 13-centimeter loaf pan
2-quart casserole	= 2-liter casserole

Temperature

212° F	= 100° C (boiling point of water)
225° F	= 110° C
250° F	= 120° C
275° F	= 135° C
300° F	= 150° C
325° F	= 160° C
350° F	= 180° C
375° F	= 190° C
400° F	= 200° C

Length

1/4 inch (in.)	= 0.6 centimeters (cm)
1/2 inch	= 1.25 centimeters
1 inch	= 2.5 centimeters

Notes

Chapter 1: Days of Darkness, Days of Light

1. Marcus Samuelsson, *Acquavit*, New York: Houghton Mifflin, 2003, p. 18.

2. Kari Diehl, "How to Prepare Gravlax," About.com, February 12, 2008, http://scandinavianfood.about.com/b/2008/02/12/how-to-prepare-gravlax.htm.

3. Samuelsson, *Acquavit*, p. 77.

4. Taimi Previdi, *The Best of Finnish Cooking*, New York: Hippocrene, 2000, p. 17.

5. Cheryl Long, ed., *The Best of Scan Fest*, Lake Oswego, OR: Culinary Arts, 1992, p. 11.

6. Beatrice Ojakangas, *Scandinavian Feasts*, Minneapolis: University of Minnesota Press, 1992, p. 5.

Chapter 2: Favorite Foods

7. Regina Schrambling, "The End of Smorrebrod?" *Saveur*, April 2006, p. 80.

8. Ojakangas, *Scandinavian Feasts*, p. 131.

9. Long, *Best of Scan Fest*, p. 9.

10. Previdi, *Best of Finnish Cooking*, p. 43.

11. Samuelsson, *Acquavit*, p. 95.

12. Beatrice Ojakangas, *Scandinavian Cooking*, Minneapolis: University of Minnesota Press, 2003, p. 13.

13. Previdi, *Best of Finnish Cooking*, p. 22.

14. Janis Andersen, "Frikadeller: Danish Meatballs," Janis Gardens, www.twentymile.com/Cookbook/frikadeller.htm.

Chapter 3: Going Out for Coffee

15. Kari Diehl, "Favorite Fika Foods," About.com, http://scandinavianfood.about.com/od/introduction/tp/Favorite-Fika-Foods.htm.

16. Scandinavian Cooking, "Cardamom," Scandinavian Cooking, http://scandinaviancooking.com/articles/cardamom.htm.

17. Ojakangas, *Scandinavian Cooking*, p. 251.

18. Kari Diehl, "Swedish Apple Cake," About.com, http://scandinavianfood.about.com/od/cakerecipes/r/applecake.htm.

19. Bibliophile, "Rjómaterta I: Cream Cake I," blog entry, About.com, March 19, 2007, http://scandinavianfood.about.com/gi/dynamic/offsite.htm?zi=1/XJ/Ya&sdn=scandinavianfood&zu=http%3A%2F%2Ficecook.blogspot.com.

20. Jerry Anne Di Vecchio, "Royal Treat: Princess Cake Recipe," *Sunset*, December 1999, http://findarticles.com/p/articles/mi_m1216/is_6_203/ai_57815362.

Chapter 4: Celebrating with Food

21. Samuelsson, *Acquavit*, p. 2.

22. Ojakangas, *Scandinavian Cooking*, p. 267.

23. Faith Adiele, "My African Sister," PBS, www.pbs.org/weta/myjourneyhome/faith/faith_sister_2.html.

24. Long, *Best of Scan Fest*, p. 112.

25. Ojakangas, *Scandinavian Cooking*, p. 178.

Glossary

appelkaka: Apple cake.

cardamom: A spice similar to ginger.

cloudberries: Yellow berries that grow in the Arctic.

cure: To preserve meat, fish, or seafood by smoking, drying, or salting it.

fika: Going out for coffee.

flatbreads: Crisp breads that have been left to dry out.

glogg: Hot, spiced punch.

gravlax: Salmon that is cured by salting.

krumkaker iron: A patterned tool used to make cookies.

krumkakers: Imprinted cone-shaped cookies.

lingonberries: Sour red berries.

lutefisk: Dried salted codfish.

marzipan: A sweet paste made from ground almonds.

pepparkakar: Ginger cookies.

plattar pan: A pan used to make pancakes.

porridges: Soft foods made by boiling grains in milk or water.

rusks: Twice-baked breads.

sillsallad: A salad made with pickled herring and beets.

smorgasbords: Large buffets of appetizer foods that lead up to the main meal.

smorrebrods: Thick open-faced sandwiches.

Vikings: Early settlers of Scandinavia, also known as Norsemen.

For Further Exploration

Books

Eric Braun, *Norway in Pictures*. Minneapolis, MN: Lerner, 2003. This simple book looks at Norway's history, geography, and culture with lots of pictures.

John James, *The Life and Times of the Vikings*. London: Kingfisher, 2007. This is an informative book about how the Vikings lived, including a chapter on food and drink.

Sylvia Munsen, *Cooking the Norwegian Way*. Minneapolis, MN: Lerner, 2002. This is a Norwegian cookbook written for younger readers.

Robert Pateman, *Denmark*. New York: Benchmark, 2006. This book focuses on Danish culture, including religion, daily life, and food.

Douglas A. Phillips, *Finland*. New York: Chelsea House, 2008. This book offers information on Finland's history, government, economics, and culture.

Jonathan Wilcox and Zawiah Abdul Latif, *Iceland*. New York: Benchmark, 2007. This book focuses on Icelandic culture, including religion, daily life, and food.

Web Sites

A to Z Kids Stuff (www.atozkidsstuff.com). This site offers educational activities for children of all ages, including an "Around the World" section that provides information about different countries, including Sweden.

Denmark.dk (www.denmark.dk). This is the official Web site of Denmark. It offers a "Meet the Kids!" section just for young people with lots of interesting and fun information about Denmark, including traditions and foods.

Iceland.org (www.iceland.org). This is a site all about Iceland. The page for the Embassy of Iceland in Washington, D.C., offers a link to "Iceland for Kids," which has information about Iceland prepared just for kids, plus many useful links.

KnowledgeBears.com (www.kbears.com). This site for young users offers games and information on animals, geography, and dinosaurs. A world map lets users click on a country in order to view statistics, history, pictures, maps, and links.

Scandinaviafood.com (www.scandinaviafood.com). This site offers recipes, articles, and information about Scandinavian cooking.

TIME for Kids (www.timeforkids.com/TFK/kids). This is the *TIME for Kids* magazine's Web site. It offers sections that help students with research, writing, and homework. In the "Around the World" section is information about different countries, including pictures, maps, folktales, time lines, and e-mail picture postcards.

The Viking Answer Lady (www.vikinganswerlady.com). This site offers all sorts of information about the Vikings and their daily life.

Index

pea soup, 22
roast beef smorrebrod, 20
strawberry cream cake, *37*, 38
reindeer meat, 26
roast beef smorrebrod recipe, 20
Rovaniemi, Finland, 43
rusks, 16
rye flour, 13–14, *14*, 16

Saint Lucia's Day, 51
salmon, cured, 7–8, 9, 48
Sami, 26
Samuelsson, Marcus
  on Christmas cookies, 42
  on gravlax, 7–8
  on mushroom foraging, 12
  on pea soup, 21–23
Santa Claus's headquarters, 43
Scandinavia, about, 4, 6
Scandinavian Cooking (Web site), 31
Schrambling, Regina, 17–19
seafood. *See* fish and seafood
sillsallad, 8, *8*
smorgasbords, 41, 48–51
smorrebrods, 17–21, *19*
soup, pea, 21–24, *23*
spices, 10, 30–31, 33
  See also dill
strawberry cream cake recipe, *37*, 38
Sweden
  gummy fish, 36, *36*
  location, 4, 5
  national dish, 23
  progressive nature of, 18
  rusks, 16
  See also Vikings

Vikings, 6
  fish and, 7
  spices and, 10, 31
vitamins and berries, 13

World War II, 18, 21

Picture Credits

About the Author

Barbara Sheen is the author of more than 50 books for young people. She lives in New Mexico with her family. In her spare time, she likes to swim, walk, garden, and read. Of course, she loves to cook!